D1013175

CANTILLON'S CURSE

Some thoughts on a world of non-neutral,
constantly expanding money supply

Stephen Johnston

To Willem, Libby and Connor, the next generation.

Copyright Stephen Johnston 2012

First Published in 2013
Second printing, 2017

Editors: Kenton Toews and Naomi Nind

ISBN: 978-0-9918375-0-2

TABLE OF CONTENTS

PROLOGUE

"Just because you do not take an interest in politics doesn't mean politics won't take an interest in you." Pericles

"There are two ways to be fooled. One is to believe what isn't true; the other is to refuse to believe what is true." Søren Kierkegaard

"People can foresee the future only when it coincides with their own wishes, and the most grossly obvious facts can be ignored when they are unwelcome." George Orwell

"Alexander Hamilton started the U.S. Treasury with nothing, and that was the closest our country has ever been to being even." Will Rogers

"When the people find that they can vote themselves money that will herald the end of the republic." Benjamin Franklin

"Economic progress is the work of the savers, who accumulate capital, and of the entrepreneurs, who turn capital to new uses. The other members of society, of course, enjoy the advantages of progress, but they not only do not contribute anything to it; they even place obstacles in its way." Ludwig von Mises

"The first requisite of a sound monetary system is that it put the least possible power over the quantity or quality of money in the hands of the politicians." Henry Hazlitt

"An economist's guess is liable to be as good as anybody else's." Will Rogers

I am not an economist by formal training or inclination, so the idea behind this book was not to produce a treatise on the causes of the financial malaise that has settled over the West, but rather to provide readers with some alternatives to mainstream views when thinking about the future.

More than anything else, this book is about my belief that the responsibility for our current problems can be laid directly at the feet of the destructive Keynesian economic thinking[1] that has taken over both the government and the financial sector and that the continuation of this Keynesian policy approach will have serious consequences for investors everywhere. In fairness, it must be said that Keynes, as opposed to his modern acolytes, did not advocate perpetual budget deficits but rather counter-cyclical deficits and surpluses. However, under cover of the belief in the utility of fiscal and monetary stimulus that Keynes certainly provided, we have devolved into a world where the choices seem to be excessive government deficits on the one hand and excessive government deficits on the other.

To persecute the professional Keynesian punditry class a bit further, I have also attempted to be honest about my economic guesses and have not cloaked them in the guise of spurious scientific certainty. In fact, I have tried to keep the use of specific data to a minimum with the view that much of it will be out of date by the time you read these pages. Events are moving so rapidly that data obsolescence is a distinct issue for anyone writing about financial topics.

What you will find in this book is a series of short quasi-independent summaries of some noteworthy trends with the hope that these encourage readers to further independent research and thought.

It will come as no surprise that we live in an era with perhaps the most highly politicized financial markets in western history. Interventions take place on a regular basis in ways that would have been deemed outrageous just a few short years ago. What has precipitated this massive increase in the presence of non-free market actors in the economy? What has changed from the so-called "great moderation" experienced in the last 3 decades? Why are we now experiencing the financial repression of zero interest rate policies ("ZIRP"), massive bail-outs of banks, insurance companies and auto companies, temporary bans on short selling - the list goes on?

Is this just a transitory phenomenon or are we witnessing the birth of something more sustained? I believe the latter. I believe monetary conditions have developed to the point of seriously damaging the foundation of our affluent western lifestyles and, unless we make appropriate preparations, they could make us all much worse off.

What to look forward to:

- Stagflation: The mal-investments of the last two decades will act as a drag on the western economies that, when combined with government deficits that increasingly are funded by money printing (an activity that historically has proven to be inflationary), creates the ideal breeding ground for stagflation[2] or perhaps alternating periods of stagnation and inflation.
- Defaults: On and off balance sheet liabilities are coming home to roost for both the state and the Finance, Insurance and Real Estate ("FIRE") sectors. The era of insolvency, both sovereign and private, is upon us.
- Emerging Markets: The West is faced with the rise of a massive savings and investment-driven competitor in the form of the emerging markets.

- Demographics: It has been said that demographics are destiny. The deterioration of western demographics presents two problems for our economies. Firstly, retiring baby boomers will be eligible for increasing amounts of social entitlements at a time when sovereign finances are in poor condition. Secondly, as boomers switch to consuming rather than accumulating capital in their retirement they will tend to exert downward pressure on investment returns, particularly in the public markets.
- Unintended Consequences: The actions by central banks that are aimed at saving the banks may inadvertently inflate hard assets and are certainly destroying the pension system.
- Energy: The ever-greater use of energy has driven population growth and wealth generation throughout history. It is the pervasive and inexpensive access to energy, combined with property rights, that created the pre-conditions for the great wealth that exists in the West. If the energy markets are moving to higher cost conditions this would present a real constraint on growth and, given the high energy inputs into virtually all commodity production, a driver for higher commodity prices in general. The result would be a transfer of wealth from commodity consumers to commodity producers.
- Agriculture: Increased demand for "food, feed and fuel" will put upward real pressure on the agricultural commodity complex.
- Financialization: The trend of financialization of the western economies will reverse as the financial sector shrinks to a more historically normal and sustainable level. Remember that the financial sector has been a large source of highly compensated white-collar professional employment in the west.

It is possible to prosper in most economic climates, however challenging, but the one into which we are heading will require a change in approach and the ability to contemplate much different sets of returns drivers than those experienced during the last three decades.

The sad fact is that, whether wittingly or unwittingly, government policies of artificially low interest rates and heavily subsidized risk have created an overhang of mal-investments in the FIRE sectors and encouraged the western economies to consume rather than produce and save. The unwinding of these trends is going to be traumatic, particularly for the middle class of the developed world.

The answer to why jobs are not coming back as quickly as compared to other post-war recoveries is the overhang of mal-investment. By keeping interest rates artificially low, our governments are making the problems worse because mal-investments are not liquidated, public debt levels increase, and further capital is destroyed by being misdirected into activities that are ultimately loss making.

Despite the propaganda from the Keynesians to the contrary, we will only see a sustainable recovery take place once free markets are able to price risk and money (interest rates), rather than this being done by government and central banker decrees.

I want to explain why I believe Austrian Economics will experience a renaissance in the years to come. Austrian Economics is much better at explaining past events and is certainly more predictive of future outcomes. Austrian Economics advocate free markets and the reduction of the role of government and it goes further to blame government interventionist policies and controlled markets as the reason for poor growth. Currently, Keynesianism is the dominant economic ideology. It is widely taught and practiced and is the mainstream media's choice of theory when discussing current affairs.

Our era of synchronized, global, fiat money[3] inflation efforts is without precedent. From the financial crisis in 2008 until 2012, the monetary base of the world's reserve currency has increased over 200%[4] and is still growing.[5] We are in the midst of some unsustainable trends; if history and Austrian Economics are a guide, then this practice will end in a crisis.

The following principle will be restated many times in this book:

> *There is no way to create capital and the prosperity that flows from it other than through private savings and private production.*

Sadly this is a message to which our governments, under the sway of Keynesian ideology, are unwilling to listen. It is axiomatic that state spending requires that capital is first taken out of the hands of profit-making private sector enterprises via taxes, borrowing or inflation and then deployed in what are often loss-making public sector activities and corporate subsidies.

To quote Jens Parssons from the *Dying of Money: Lessons of the Great German & American Inflations*:

> *Everyone loves an early inflation. The effects at the beginning of inflation are all good. There is steepened money expansion, rising government spending, increased government budget deficits, booming stock markets, and spectacular general prosperity, all in the midst of temporarily stable prices.* **Everyone benefits, and no-one pays.** *That is the early part of the cycle. In the later inflation, on the other hand, the effects are all bad. The government may steadily increase the money inflation in order to stave off the latter effects, but the latter effects patiently wait. In the terminal inflation, there is faltering prosperity, tightness of money, falling stock markets, rising taxes, still larger government deficits, and still roaring money expansion, now accompanied by soaring prices and an ineffectiveness of all traditional remedies.* **Everyone pays and no one benefits. That is the full cycle of every inflation.** (Emphasis mine)

The Austrian School disavows such practices, taking a laissez faire approach to the economy including monetary policy. The Austrian theory of credit as the principal driver of most business cycles holds that central banks' expansionary policies, by forcing interest rates to artificially low levels, facilitate excessive money and credit creation and discourage savings. With the increase in money supply, an artificial expansion takes place with newly created funds pursuing a pool of increasingly marginal investment opportunities.

The result is an overhang of mal-investments – or more explicitly capital misallocated into sectors and assets that would not attract investment if the money supply remained stable. Once this condition is in place the Austrians believe:

- A collapse in the price of the mal-investments is simply a matter of time; or
- If the central bank attempts to suppress the losses and support prices through continued monetary expansion then the currency itself may collapse.

As to why any rational government would pursue such destructive policies, Friedrich Hayek, the Nobel Prize-winning Austrian economist said: *"I do not think it is an exaggeration to say history is largely a history of inflation, usually inflations engineered by governments for the gain of governments."* You can bring this quote up to date by adding the financial sector as the other beneficiary. Give this some thought as you watch the governments of the world pursue their current fiscal and monetary policies.

Of course, if you insist on listening to the public comments of western central bankers you would not think that any of the aforementioned even represents a problem. However, central bankers and politicians have an incentive to provide nothing but bland assurances to the public. Let us take a look at the always entertaining if not particularly prescient Ben Bernanke, Chairman of the Federal Reserve, speaking about the US housing market over the years:

> *"We've never had a decline in house prices on a nationwide basis. So, what I think what is more likely is that house prices will slow, maybe stabilize, might slow consumption spending a bit. I don't think it's gonna drive the economy too far from its full employment path, though."* July 1, 2005

> *"Housing markets are cooling a bit. Our expectation is that the decline in activity or the slowing in activity will be moderate, that house prices will probably continue to rise."* February 15, 2006

> *"At this juncture . . . the impact on the broader economy and financial markets of the problems in the subprime markets seems likely to be contained,"* March 28, 2007

> *"While rising delinquencies and foreclosures will continue to weigh heavily on the housing market this year, it will not cripple the U.S."* May 17, 2007

> (the subprime fallout) *"will not affect the economy overall."* June 20, 2007

> *"It is not the responsibility of the Federal Reserve – nor would it be appropriate – to protect lenders and investors from the consequences of their financial decisions."* October 15, 2007

> *"I expect there will be some failures. I don't anticipate any serious problems of that sort among the large internationally active banks that make up a very substantial part of our banking system."* February 29, 2008

> *"Despite a recent spike in the nation's unemployment rate, the danger that the economy has fallen into a "substantial downturn" appears to have waned."* June 9, 2008

> (Freddie Mac and Fannie Mae)[6] *"...will make it through the storm", "... in no danger of failing.", "...adequately capitalized"* July 16, 2008

> *"most severe financial crisis"* in the post-World War II era. Investment banks are seeing *"tremendous runs on their cash,"* *"Without action, they will fail soon."* September 19, 2008

Bearing in mind his unimpressive track record predicting the housing collapse, Bernanke's response in 2011 when asked how confident he was that he could control inflation given the amount by which he was expanding the money supply and the Federal Reserve's balance sheet, was: *"One hundred percent"*. We shall see.

One last matter before we begin in earnest: Who is Cantillon and what is his "curse"? Richard Cantillon was an Irish economist born in the 1680s. He became a successful banker before he began his speculation in John Law's Mississippi Company during the late 1710s and early 1720s. It was in the growth and collapse of the Mississippi Company, and along with it the

French economy, where Cantillon was able to witness first hand the devastating effects of unbridled money printing.

Much of what is known about Cantillon comes from his book *"Essai Sur La Nature Du Commerce En Général",* which deals with, among other topics, the origins of wealth and price formation in the market and in particular Cantillon's theory of relative inflation (now known as the Cantillon Effect). The Cantillon Effect is elegant and simple to understand. At its core is the idea that inflation does not happen in the aggregate. As money is printed, purchasing power is transferred to those who receive the freshly-printed money first from those who receive it later (the purchasing power of the money falls over the long term as the supply is increased).

Since 1971, when the US defaulted on its last gold redemption obligations,[7] we have been witnessing the non-neutral effect of money printing – with the state and its proxies in the politically favored FIRE sectors being the beneficiaries. Since the dot.com market crisis in 2001, this process has been accelerating. As it progresses, increasing amounts of capital are stealthily taken from "inflatees" for the benefit of the "inflators". As a result, we are now living in a global market in the throes of the negative effects of non-neutral money printing...or what I like to call Cantillon's curse, a world where certain privileged groups are silently misappropriating the wealth of the middle classes.

CHAPTER 1:
PRINTING MONEY IN A LOW GROWTH ENVIRONMENT = STAGFLATION

"There is no subtler, no surer means of overturning the existing basis of society than to debauch the currency. The process engages all the hidden forces of economic law on the side of destruction, and does it in a manner which not one man in a million can diagnose."
John Maynard Keynes

"Cash for Clunkers - What we came up to replace World War II as stimulus. Many perfectly good cars destroyed, no Nazis defeated."
Cliff Asness

"Quantitative Easing - The act of printing pieces of paper to purchase other pieces of paper and thinking it matters at all for anything. See "dogs chasing cars" for related examples." Cliff Asness

"Gold is money. Everything else is credit." J.P. Morgan[8]

It is axiomatic that central banks can control interest rates or exchange rates[9] but not both. As of late, they are falling over themselves to signal their willingness to sacrifice exchange rates. Let there be no doubt on this point, central banks have an unblemished track record in only one area and that sadly, is currency devaluation. Here are just two examples: the US dollar has experienced a roughly 97% loss in purchasing power since the inception of the Federal Reserve and the Canadian dollar a roughly 95% loss since the inception of the Bank of Canada.[10] Clearly central bankers are operating under a different understanding of the phrase "price stability" than the rest of us.

If you want a graphic depiction of a central bank's ability to stabilize prices, look no further than the efforts to recover the SS Gairsoppa. The Gairsoppa was sunk in 1941 by a German submarine. Among its cargo was 7 million ounces of silver worth approximately US$ 2.5 million at the time. The 2012 value of the silver is approximately US$ 210 million. Would anyone even bother trying to recover the contents if the ship had been carrying US$ 2.5 million in non-redeemable paper currency instead?

Official wisdom is that a devaluation of the currency driven by low interest rates is necessary for the West to grow out of the current recession. Unfortunately, the US is pursuing this policy at the same time that most exporting nations (the majority of the World) that run a current account surplus with the US are trying to maintain export competitiveness via their own devaluation programs. ZIRP is a virtually global phenomenon. In the category of truth being stranger than fiction we even have the beginnings of negative interest rate policies or "NIRP"[11]. In June 2012 the Danish Central Bank announced that it was implementing NIRP on certificates of deposit to curb strength in the Danish currency.

Before you dismiss this as some strange northern European monetary disorder, there are historical precedents for this sort of behaviour closer to home. From 1936 to 1945, the Canadian province of Alberta was in default on its provincial debt, managing only partial coupon payments and no principal repayments. Out of cash and out of options, Alberta did what every bankrupt EU country wishes it could do: it started printing its own currency called Alberta Prosperity Certificates ("APCs"). The APCs were introduced in August 1936 and were used to pay government bills. Under the plan, the recipient of the APC was required to purchase a stamp equal to 1% of the face value of the certificates each week. The stamps had to be placed on the back of the APCs for them to be valid. For bearers of the APC, the result was that they experienced a 50% loss of purchasing power during the course of a year if they failed to spend them. Voila, NIRP!

Surely, if anything signals the desire and intention of a monetary authority to destroy the purchasing power of its currency, NIRP has to be at the very top of the list.

So, with endemic ZIRP and perhaps even episodes of NIRP on the horizon, an era of competitive currency devaluations is upon us. The consequences will be a global loss of purchasing power in all currencies or what we commonly refer to as inflation. US policy does beg the simple question - if people could be made wealthy by debasing the currency, wouldn't the Argentineans and the Zimbabweans (fill in your favourite currency failure here) be the richest people on the planet?

I would argue that, at the margin, the connection between the supply of money and its purchasing power is not complicated. The central banks of the West are printing record amounts of money and western governments are running record fiscal deficits. Simply put, we can expect our money to buy less in the future. The key is to realize that Cantillon was correct: assets do not inflate or deflate uniformly and that the collapse in the price of historically overleveraged and cash-flow challenged real-estate assets is not the same as a truly deflationary monetary environment. You can have assets falling in value even in an inflationary world.

Now you could superimpose lots of complicated jargon about low cost imports, exchange rates, productivity, technology paradigm shifts, deflation etc., but the simple truth is that something whose supply is continually increased at zero cost will decline in relative value against other goods. Therefore, as the supply of money increases, its value tends to decrease. This is commonly referred to as a reduction in purchasing power or inflation. Let's engage in some simple Q & A:

- Q: "But don't the official statistics show low inflation?"
  A: Government inflation data deliberately under-report inflation via a myriad of techniques such as "hedonic adjustments" and "rental yield equivalents". Governments have an incentive to underreport inflation for a number of reasons, including the inflation indexing components of many state pensions (lower inflation reduces state pension liabilities). In more entertaining terms, this incentive has been explained as: *"Never ask the barber if you need a haircut. Never ask the realtor if the house you are considering buying is a bargain at the price offered. And never ask the government to calculate the rate of inflation when it can save millions of dollars in cost-of-living adjustments."* [12]

- Q: "But isn't inflation necessary; wouldn't deflation destroy the economy?"
  A: Prior to the advent of fiat currencies, the general historical trend was for the price all goods and services to remain stable or even fall in real terms – falling price levels do not matter as long as your purchasing power is the same and you are not in debt. It is government money supply increases that silently erode your purchasing power.

- Q: "But don't we need a lower currency to grow our way out of the recession?"
  A: Currency devaluations do not make a country more wealthy because they do not create capital – an anonymous wag in the foreign exchange markets is reputed to have said: *"Paper currencies don't float, they just all sink at different rates"*. A falling currency simply reduces your purchasing power and makes you less wealthy in real terms.

This era of synchronized, global fiat money inflation is without precedent and is having unprecedented effects. At the time of writing, the monetary base of the world's reserve currency, the US dollar, has increased at one of the fastest paces in its history.

Once again, there is no way to create capital and the prosperity that flows from it other than through private savings and private production – printing money does not create capital. Sadly, this is a message to which our governments, under the sway of Keynesian ideology, are unwilling to listen.

I argue that history would support the observation that Big Government = Big Inflation & Low Growth. In this spirit it needs to be noted that US Federal government spending has grown seven times faster than real median household income over the last 40 years. And this is using the government's own understated inflation numbers. Government spending cannot outstrip private sector income indefinitely unless the government plans to default or inflate away its obligations. What is happening to Greece, Ireland, UK, Italy, and Spain is a microcosm of the issue that most western governments will face in the future: how to deal with impaired and deteriorating balance sheets. Some sample statistics as of 2012:

- US fiscal deficit nearly 10% of GDP - largest since WWII;

- US expects to borrow around US$ 5 trillion over the next 5 years in circumstances where there is only approximately US$ 15 trillion in existence; and
- EU and US net liabilities are estimated to exceed US$ 200 trillion – several times the capitalization of the world's equity markets. [13]

Assuming that governments accept the principle that debts must be repaid, then their options are spending less, increasing taxation, and/or printing money (inflation). I would argue that the only way debts of the magnitude set out above will be repaid is by a money supply driven inflation/currency devaluation because it is the most politically expedient in the short-term.

There is a view that government spending is stimulating and saving the economy from an even worse downturn. However, as noted by Winston Churchill: *"for a nation to tax itself into prosperity is like a man standing in a bucket and trying to lift himself up by the handle."* It could be said with equal certainty that printing and spending money as a path to prosperity falls into the same category.

Unfortunately, it seems that the only consistent skill governments and central banks possess is the ability to debauch their currencies. Granted, pointing out the role of governments and central banks in currency devaluation is not a novel observation. Many have made this connection before and much more elegantly, such as Ludwig von Mises who said: "*Government is the only institution that can take a valuable commodity like paper and make it worthless by applying ink*" and Voltaire, a man who lived through a spectacular fiat money collapse in 1720 in France, who said: *"paper money eventually returns to its intrinsic value - zero."*

You might ask: Why state the obvious? There is much talk about quantitative easing (QE), stimulus, bond yields, risk premiums, volatility, velocity of money, deflating asset prices and so on. My point is that to focus on what is happening in the immediate term is to miss the forest for the trees. Only by taking a step back is it possible to remember that the developed world is still in the midst of a truly massive and unprecedented Keynesian experiment – printing and dispensing money on a vast scale. Some say it will have no effect because the velocity of money has collapsed while others predict hyperinflation.

In the midst of all the seemingly contradictory data and the clearly contradictory predictions, I prefer, once again, to fall back on the simple economic dictum that if a good or service can be created at zero cost and is created in ever increasing quantities, its value will trend to zero. Is money subject to different rules than other goods and services? That leads directly to my next question – will the governments of the West continue to create money in ever increasing quantities?

I believe the answer to that question is yes. Eliminate the impossible (debt repayment in real terms, massive tax increases and/or a reduction in the absolute size of government) and what is left, however improbable, is what will happen – a printing press default.

In a research piece proclaiming the US is *"broke"* and that no conceivable combination of austerity and/or tax increases will fix the problem, Morgan Stanley predicted that some form of default via the printing press is sure to happen.[14] In research of a similar vein, Société Générale (SocGen) went a step further and calculated the approximate net worth of various western governments. To use SocGen's circumspect language: *"the fiscal challenges are unprecedented"*. More specifically SocGen concluded that Italy, Germany, France, Portugal, United States, the United Kingdom, Spain, Ireland and Greece all have large negative net worth and are only avoiding default because, thanks to massive central bank intervention, they are still able to roll maturing debt and pay the historically low interest on their outstanding debt. By the time you read this it is possible that one or more of the countries on this list may have proven unable even to do this any longer.

It is the unfolding bankruptcy of western governments that will drive inflation as they increasingly rely on the printing presses to fund their deficits. It has been observed that:

> *Hyperinflation is a fiscal not a monetary phenomenon. The reality is that hyperinflation is first and foremost set in motion and driven by a deteriorating fiscal situation. In fact, significant economic weakness and deflation is a precursor to hyperinflation. Too many analysts believe that there has to be some economic demand or some consumption to stimulate inflation or hyperinflation. Printing money to try and stimulate your economy or excessive credit growth is what leads to inflation.* **Printing money because you are broke and can't service your debts is what leads to hyperinflation.**[15] (Emphasis mine)

Following the catastrophic experience in the Weimar Republic, central bankers in large western economies once had a visceral reluctance to engage in unbridled money printing. Now they have crossed the money printing Rubicon, so to speak. Dylan Grice of SocGen performed an interesting review of the Weimar Republic inflation. Apparently, economic thought at the time held that increasing the money supply had nothing to do with the rate of inflation. Instead, Germans were told the war reparations Germany had to pay caused the high rates of inflation. As a result, Prussian central banker Rudolf von Havenstein felt able to monetize Germany's debt during and following the First World War. Grice wrote:

> *Surely we understand what happens when deficits are financed with printed money, and that it is only backward and corrupt states that don't know any better, like Bolivia and Zimbabwe? ...*
>
> *And anyway, how could Von Havenstein not have known that the continued and escalating printing of money to fund government deficits would cause inflation? The United States experience of unrestrained money printing during the Civil War had been well documented, as had the hyperinflation of revolutionary France in the late 18th century.*
> *...*
>
> **The fact is we do understand the economics of inflation.** *Despite what economists everywhere say about being in "uncharted territory" with QE,* **we know that if you keep monetizing deficits eventually you get inflation,** *and we know that once you're on that path it can be extremely difficult to get off it. But we knew that then. The real problem is that inflation is an inherently political variable and that concern over debt sustainability and unfunded welfare obligations leaves us more dependent on politicians than we have been in many decades.*[16] (Emphasis mine)

Even with all the historical examples, do the people running central banks today understand where inflation comes from? Federal Reserve Governor Janet Yellen said, in support of her view that the Fed's role is to create full employment: *"If it were possible to take [nominal] interest rates into* **negative territory***, I would be voting for that."* (Emphasis mine)

Once again, I adhere to the school of thought that fiat currency is like any other commodity – at the most basic level its price is ultimately dictated by supply and demand. It is on the question of supply that the most disputes occur. Is the supply of fiat currency increasing or decreasing – i.e. do we inhabit an inflationary or deflationary world? I believe the Austrian School of Economics provides the most useful measure of money supply: known simply as the True Money Supply ("TMS"). TMS was formulated by Murray Rothbard and represents the amount of money in the economy that is available for immediate use in exchange. It has been referred to in the past as the Austrian Money Supply, the Rothbard Money Supply and the True Money Supply. The full technical definition for those interested can be found in the bibliography.[17]

Regardless of the specifics of the construction of TMS, suffice it to say I believe it is a more accurate reflection of the money supply and it continues to grow rapidly. Such growth is inflationary.

It is important not to confuse the collapse of prices of leveraged assets (caused by insufficient cash generating qualities to service the debt) as "deflation". As Cantillon demonstrated, inflation is not an aggregate or neutral phenomenon – the presence of deleveraging and falling asset prices in certain parts of the economy is not evidence of deflation and does not negate the effect of increases in the money supply. Instead, the increase tends not to have any effect in these over-leveraged asset classes but rather works to inflate nominal prices in other areas of the economy. I believe you can have rapidly falling and increasing nominal prices in an inflationary world, particularly when extremely high leverage exists in select areas of the economy.

Still not convinced we inhabit an inflationary world? If you calculate the US Consumer Price Index ("CPI") using the pre-1980s methodology, as Shadowstats.com does, you can see that inflation is approaching levels not seen since the 1970s when the US last lost control of monetary policy. Shawdowstats states: *"In general terms, methodological shifts in government reporting have depressed reported inflation, moving the concept of the CPI away from being a measure of the cost of living needed to maintain a constant standard of living."* [18] Remember the prior mention of hedonic adjustments and rental yield equivalents? The idea now is that as goods become more expensive we substitute less expensive items – e.g. steak replaced with hamburger. So in effect, US CPI is kept low with the implicit assumption of a declining standard of living.

Clearly inflation in the purest sense is not running at subdued levels in the US or anywhere else for that matter – at least not for those of us trying to maintain our standard of living.

To follow the logic of this chapter to its conclusion, if the banking system and more importantly the governments of the West are technically bankrupt and already engaging in rapid money supply growth, then isn't a printing press inflationary default plausible as the way for them to exit this morass? Time will tell, but I feel certain about this: governments and central banks will continue to print money. They may try to disguise this fact for political reasons but they appear to be reaching the point of no return.

CHAPTER 2:
THE ERA OF SOVEREIGN INSOLVENCY

"I am a rich man, as long as I do not pay my creditors."
Titus Maccius Plautus

"Blessed are the young for they shall inherit the national debt."
Herbert Hoover

"I don't make jokes. I just watch the government and report the facts." Will Rogers

"Men prefer a false promise to a flat refusal." Quintus Cicero

Another burst of sovereign insolvency appears to be well underway. Sovereign borrowers have had unlimited borrowing privileges over the last two decades – a privilege they used, or perhaps abused, with abandon. Those privileges are being revoked as the ability to repay is being called into doubt. Without the ability to roll over their obligations, the truly precarious nature of sovereign finances is being revealed. Consider that while interest rates for many developed nations are at generational lows, sovereign debt loads as a percentage of GDP are at all time highs.

What happens to western governments when their borrowing costs go from 2% to something approaching the long-term historical average of between 5% to 6%? In the US, the answer is that the majority of the budget would be dedicated to simply paying interest.

Perhaps this sounds alarmist and unlikely. But consider that, as of 2012, US federal government debt exceeds US$ 15 trillion. In 2011, the US government paid US$ 454 billion in interest (an implied rate of 2.9%). According to the Congressional Budget Office, federal government debt will rise to US$ 20 trillion by 2015. If we assume that it carried a rate of 5% instead of 3%, interest payments would total US$ 1 trillion or 45% of current tax revenues.

Unfortunately, these debt numbers understate the issue significantly. It is estimated that the present value of all future US expenditures (including such items as social entitlements and pensions etc.) less all currently contemplated future tax revenues, amounts to over a US$ 200 trillion deficit.[19] Now imagine this is funded with debt carrying 5% interest, then the annual interest bills would be US$ 10 trillion or 500% of current tax revenues.

The day of reckoning cannot be postponed indefinitely. Maturing sovereign debt must be refinanced, creating what is commonly referred to as rollover risk. Rollover risk can be defined broadly as the possibility that a borrower cannot refinance maturing debt. If combined with insufficient funds/liquid assets on hand to fund the shortfall, the borrower will experience a liquidity problem and technically be considered insolvent.

Here is a concrete example of rollover risk that may be unfolding right in front of us. By 2015, it is estimated that US$ 15 trillion (50%) of the debt of the top 10 global debtors will have matured and must be rolled over. Considering that global GDP is estimated at US$ 70 trillion, the magnitude of this number begs the questions: how will this maturing debt be re-financed and, perhaps more importantly, at what interest rates?

Although the US bond market seems well bid for now (courtesy of the US Federal Reserve), private lenders are retreating from peripheral markets at the first hint of trouble. If this continues, either the monetary authorities will have to step in and monetize all forms of maturing debt or interest rates will have to rise considerably from current historic lows. We are seeing the outcome of this process on a relatively modest scale in southern EU countries - what would happen if it went global?

I believe politicians are starting to sense the rollover end game is underway; hence the terror around keeping interest rates low by having central banks intervene in the bond market. Given the circumstances, expect these interventions, and hence currency debasement, to continue.

CHAPTER 3:
DEMOGRAPHICS ARE DESTINY

"There is a kind of fear, approaching a panic, that's spreading through the Baby Boom Generation, which has suddenly discovered that it will have to provide for its own retirement." Ron Chernow

"The United States is facing an untenable fiscal situation due to the combination of high fiscal deficits, an aging population and rapid growth in government-provided healthcare benefits. IMF and Congressional Budget Office forecasts imply that U.S. debt will rise rapidly relative to GDP in the medium to long term." IMF[20]

"The debt problem facing advanced economies is even worse than we thought… Debt is rising to points that are above anything we have seen, except during major wars. Public debt ratios are currently on an explosive path in a number of countries. These countries will need to implement drastic policy changes. Stabilization might not be enough." Bank for International Settlements[21]

The West is facing a wave of retirements as the Baby Boom generation moves to the end of their productive careers. The Baby Boom generation is defined as those people born between 1946 and 1964 according to the US Census Bureau. The magnitude of this trend is undeniable.

In 2000, the ratio of Americans between 15 and 59 years old to those over 60 was four to one, according to a United Nations report. In 2050, the ratio will be only two to one. In Canada the story is much the same. By approximately 2015, Canada will have more people leaving the labour force than joining. Retirees are expected to exceed 40% of the Canadian working age population by the mid-2010s.[22] I believe this will have some serious consequences:

- Returns: Lower future returns on western financial assets will require more pension contributions for the same level of retirement income. From 1946 through 1997, stocks had an average compound annual return of 7.5% after inflation. Robert Schiller, author of *Irrational Exuberance*, argues that returns over the next 20 years could fall below 5% after inflation as price-earnings ratios move back toward their long-term mean.

- Retirement Funding: As they retire, this large and affluent cohort will begin to realize that the government will not be there to bail them out; therefore, they will attempt to increase their savings. It must be said that, eventually, the return to a savings-driven economy will be a good development but the transition will be painful.

- Investment Liquidation: The West is generally moving into a phase where investments are liquidated to fund retirements. As Baby Boomers retire they will begin to sell assets, producing downward pricing pressure in some key markets – residential real estate, government bonds and public equities. This is where Baby Boomer's investment capital has been focused for two decades. Unfortunately, we cannot all cash out at once.

- Pension Solvency: The solvency of both public and private pension plans will be tested and I believe that in many cases found to be lacking. The combination of ZIRP, unrealistic return assumptions and the rapid growth in the pool of recipients will see to this. In the event that there are wide-scale funding shortfalls in pensions and social programs what can we expect governments to do? I believe that they will be loathe to cut entitlements and so will have to borrow or print to fund the gaps.

The emerging markets in aggregate will not face our demographic challenge for several decades. The emerging markets currently have a dependency ratio (the ratio of dependents to working-age citizens) roughly equal to the developed markets. However, this overlooks the composition of the dependents:

> *According to the United Nations, the current dependency ratio is about even at 62% for both developing and developed nations. An important difference between developing and developed countries is the type of dependents: The majority of non-workers in developed countries are past the working age; the majority of non-workers in developing countries are not yet old enough to enter the workforce.* **Based on the United Nations' projection of demographic trends to 2050, emerging countries are poised to gain a substantial advantage over developed ones.**[23] (Emphasis mine)

This demographic advantage is expected to emerge quite soon - by 2016, the dependency ratio in developed markets will be higher than that of emerging markets and growing faster.[24]

The process I am describing here is already well underway. If you do not believe me, here is the analysis from the US Federal Reserve – an organization which is much more likely to err on the side of optimism in such matters:

> *Historical data indicate a strong relationship between the age distribution of the U.S. population and stock market performance. A key demographic trend is the aging of the baby boom generation. As they reach retirement age, they are likely to shift from buying stocks to selling their equity holdings to finance retirement. .... P/E* should decline persistently from about 15 in 2010 to about 8.4 in 2025, before recovering to 9.14 in 2030.... Moreover, the demographic changes related to the retirement of the baby boom generation are well known. This suggests that market participants may anticipate that equities will perform poorly in the future, an expectation that can potentially depress current stock prices. In that sense, these demographic shifts may present headwinds today for the stock market's recovery from the financial crisis.* [25]

Why am I devoting all this space to demographics and the Baby Boom retirement wave? It leads to the key demographic sore point in the West - pension finances. ZIRP and other expansionary monetary policies are effectively throwing pension plans and other savers onto the bonfire of the banking system. What I mean by this is that low interest rates have created a huge stealth subsidy for the banking system at the cost of those who actually saved for retirement.

The issue for pensions arises because a significant number assume annual returns in the range of 7%-8% when they are planning how to meet their obligations. Since a large portion of pension portfolios are in fixed income securities that are now yielding a fraction of that range, these return assumptions are farcical to put it mildly. The longer ZIRP continues, the worse the problem will become. Ultimately, benefits will have to be reduced and/or large amounts of additional capital in the form of higher contributions will have to be collected. Barring this, pensions will need bail-outs or go bankrupt.

Just how serious is this funding shortfall? A recent pair of studies[26] concluded that the unfunded obligations of US municipal pensions were more than double the officially reported figures. By the municipalities' accounting, they had approximately US$ 200 billion in unfunded obligations while the study put the actual amount at approximately US$ 400 billion. The state-funding gap was projected to be over US$ 3 trillion for a grand total at the municipal and state levels of around US$ 3.5 trillion. More generally, as of the 2010 accounting rules, US public pension plans had 76 cents for every dollar they must pay retirees in the future. If more realistic mark-to-market[27] of assets took place combined with lower long-term return assumptions, this number could drop to as low as 57 cents.[28]

Private sector pensions are also in poor condition. In Canada, 92% of private sector pension plans were in a deficit position as of December 31, 2008, with almost 40% of defined benefit plans having solvency ratios under 70%, and over 70% of defined benefit plans having solvency ratios under 80%.[29] As of 2008, total defined benefit and defined contribution plan assets amounted to approximately CAD$ 600 billion and the estimated funding shortfall was CAD$ 350 billion. Put into perspective, that is 58% unfunded.[30]

In the US at the end of 2011, the companies in the S&P 500 had pension plan obligations of US$ 1.68 trillion and assets of US$ 1.32 trillion. The shortfall of US$ 355 billion was the largest ever reported.[31] Without excess contributions by plan sponsors, it remains to be seen how these shortfalls can be made up in a low equity return and ZIRP environment.

Meanwhile, retirees who have been promised benefits are going to exert powerful political pressure to be paid in full. Unfortunately, it does not appear that there will be enough cash to pay them and stay solvent. Once again, the government is likely to step in and bail out the pension system with more freshly-printed money. But what will this money be worth in real terms?

Chapter 4:
The Law of Unintended Consequences

"If government had taken over the auto industry in 1920, today we'd all be driving Model-T cars -- and saying, 'If it weren't for the government, we'd have no cars at all.'" Harry Browne

"If a government were put in charge of the Sahara Desert, within five years they'd have a shortage of sand." Dr. Milton Friedman

"If a politician found he had cannibals among his constituents, he would promise them missionaries for dinner." H. L. Mencken

"The whole aim of practical politics is to keep the populace alarmed (and hence clamorous to be led to safety) by menacing it with an endless series of hobgoblins, all of them imaginary." H. L. Mencken

"With the continuous firming of the Chinese Yuan, the US dollar is fast ceasing to be the world's reserve currency and the Euro-Zone debt crisis has made things even worse." Gideon Gono, Governor of the Central Bank of Zimbabwe

"The art of taxation consists in so plucking the goose as to obtain the largest possible amount of feathers with the smallest possible amount of hissing." Jean Baptiste Colbert

Allow me to begin with two generalizations:

- All actions have unintended consequences; and
- Path dependence can become your enemy.

Overly-specific predictions about the future are bound to be incorrect. Perhaps, however, it is possible to determine what is not likely to happen based on the options available. Of course the options open to us today reflect and are circumscribed by the decisions we have made in the past, both good and bad - a concept otherwise known as path dependence.

Using path dependence as our model, let us ask an important question: Is it possible for the West to achieve sustainable real growth with expanding fiscal deficits, enormous unrecognized future liabilities, largely insolvent banking and pension systems, and unrestrained monetary growth?

I believe the answer is yes but we still must determine: 1) the most appropriate path to take us to this desired outcome; and 2) how likely is that path to be taken given our current situation?

I would argue that all minimally disruptive paths are now closed due to the massive imbalances that central banks and governments – let us call them non-profit maximizers ("NPMs") – have created in the economy. I realize this may seem like a heretical viewpoint to some but NPMs magnify rather than reduce system instability as they are indifferent to losses and they allow risk to accumulate through hidden and, more recently, explicit subsidies, such as when the Fed started buying mortgage-backed securities in September 2012. Because the path to sustainable growth threatens the status quo, NPMs are willing to continue with current risk increasing activities – the quintessential postponing of the day of reckoning.

Unfortunately, this behaviour has turned the economy into the ultimate version of an unstable sand pile. The only decision that the NPMs seem interested in making is whether or not to add more grains of sand to the pile in the form of newly-printed money. This answer is apparently always "yes". The longer such a system continues, the more unstable it becomes. At some point, adding merely one additional grain of sand can cause unpredictable and catastrophic avalanches to occur with no way to predict this in advance.

To continue with the metaphor, perhaps our recent stock-market crashes are simply the financial world's version of avalanches in an increasingly unstable system. If you do not believe me, let us quickly examine the global economic sand pile and attendant avalanches that our NPMs have inflicted on us over the last decade, each one on average bigger than its predecessor:

NPM Action: Suppress interest rates/increase money supply

Results: Newly-printed money flowed into the public equity markets

- Dot-com bubble
- Dot-com crash

NPM Action: Suppress interest rates/increase money supply

Results: Newly-printed money flowed into the real estate markets

- Subsidize real estate risk, causing bubble

- Banks package subsidized real estate risk via a range of financial instruments - e.g. REITS, Residential Mortgage Backed Securities ("RMBS"), Commercial Mortgage Backed Securities ("CMBS")
- Rating agencies give these securities AAA investment status
- Real estate prices begin reversion to mean
- Real estate financial instruments are materially overvalued, mark-to-market forces banks to book huge losses
- Banks insolvent

NPM Action: Suppress interest rates/increase money supply

Results: Newly-printed money flows into the bond markets

- Bond yields are driven lower – real interest rates go negative
- Negative real interest rates drive commodity prices higher – particularly precious metals, energy and food
- High energy prices act as tax on energy import dependent economies and offset the low interest rate subsidies created by NPMs
- Increasing energy prices cause western current account deficits to worsen, putting downward pressure on currencies
- Newly-printed money flows into emerging economies where inflation rises due to currency pegs
- Inflation, particularly rising food prices, causes political instability in emerging economies – unrest in key oil producing regions creates more upward pressure on oil prices
- Low interest rate policies cause pension-funding shortfalls in the West, pension funding shortfalls will have to be back-stopped by the state increasing future debt levels – putting downward pressure on currencies
- Low interest rates meant to support asset prices in the FIRE economy negatively affect the middle classes via commodity inflation and the virtual elimination of passive interest income
- Artificially low interest rates force central banks to step in to replace increasingly reluctant private bond investors and purchase large amounts of incremental sovereign debt issuance - more downward pressure on currencies and upward pressure on commodities
- Investors, concerned about growing sovereign debt and systemic risk, increasingly prefer to move newly-printed money outside of the paper based financial system directly into commodities and other real assets

Let us return to our path problem - how does the West return to sustained, real growth? The simple answer is to stop adding to the sand pile. Stop printing money, reduce the size of government and stop subsidizing risk in the financial sector. Only this will return us to sustainable growth. All of the other solutions being bruited about are merely economic equivalents of adding grains to the increasingly unstable sand pile. Is this change likely to happen? I believe we are at the point where the entrenched interests of the NPMs and the banking system would rather risk a collapse than accept any necessary economic restructuring. So they will continue to add sand until the "avalanche" is too big and destructive to be ignored.

Is it ridiculous to assume that this reckless behaviour could cause a developed world currency to collapse? According to a study of the 775 fiat currencies that have existed, 599 are no longer in circulation.[32] Moreover, the average life span of a fiat currency is only 34 years. The median is even less encouraging at only 15 years. Only a select few have managed anything approaching old age.

The British pound sterling is one such example at over 300 years and counting. Before we get too excited by this apparent example of longevity, at inception the pound was worth 12 ounces of silver and now it is worth less than 0.5% of this original value. In other words, the most successful currency in existence in terms of life span has lost more than 99% of its value. The study also found that 1 in 5 fiat currencies have failed outright through hyper-inflation – a percentage that I must admit surprised me because I was under the impression that hyperinflation was a much less common occurrence.

I think it is safe to assume that the monetary authorities in the countries referenced in the study did not intend for their currencies to fail – rather the failure flowed as an unintended consequence of their misguided policies. Such policies typically revolved around the use of the printing press in an attempt to prevent market forces from acting – whether on government debt or on politically favoured but insolvent segments of the economy - public pension plans, banks etc.

Regardless how it happens, it certainly appears that fiat currencies have a pronounced tendency to fail in *de jure* or at least in *de facto* terms with time being the only relevant variable. Some argue that fiat issued by a dominant economic/military power is the exception to this rule – e.g. the pound sterling or the US dollar. While this status certainly seems to extend the life span of a fiat currency, this conclusion surely misses the point that a relentless loss of purchasing power is just a failure in slow motion.

Since one of the key requirements of money is to act as a store of value and fiat currency seems abysmal at this function, why do we persist in its use and, more importantly, who benefits? The answer is obvious – fiat currency is extremely useful to the ones who create it, not to those who are forced to use it.

For politicians, printing money acts as a stealth tax – a tax for which few voters are likely to blame the political class. Secondly, by reducing the value of the currency, the economy's "measuring stick", politicians are able to deceive the voters that their wealth has increased because of the nominal increase in asset prices.

Meanwhile, members of the banking class are ideally positioned to take advantage of the confusion between the nominal and real value of the country's capital (the "measuring stick" issue again). In simple terms, they can strategically and quickly exchange a declining currency for productive assets because they are able to deploy the currency before its loss is realized, all while artificially low interest rates act to subsidize their activities. Secondly, through their direct influence over the money printing authorities they socialize losses and privatize gains – aka bailouts.

So the answer to the question "why print money?" is simple. For certain privileged participants, a significant amount of wealth can be quietly and almost effortlessly misappropriated. For the rest of us, the expansion of the money supply offers no true benefits and instead exposes us to the very real danger of our wealth being misappropriated.

Ludwig Von Mises prophetically wrote: *"There is no means of avoiding the final collapse of a boom brought about by credit expansion. The alternative is only whether the crisis should come sooner, as the result of a voluntary abandonment of further credit expansion, or later, as a final and total catastrophe of the currency system involved."*

I believe we will continue to see negative unintended consequences as long as NPMs are determined to thwart the free market, perhaps to the fatal point mentioned by Mises: *"A final and total catastrophe of the currency system."*

Chapter 5:
Energy – The Onset of Difficult Oil

"Anyone who believes exponential growth can go on forever in a finite world is either a madman or an economist." Kenneth Boulding

The global average decline rate of post-peak fields is at least 6.5%/year and the corresponding decline rate of all currently producing fields is at least 4%/year. This implies that approximately 3 million barrels/day of capacity must be added each year. UKERC[33]

Just to maintain production at current levels is the equivalent to a new Saudi Arabia coming on-stream every 3 years and an additional 1 million barrels/day must be added to meet demand growth. UKERC[34]

More than two thirds of existing capacity must be replaced by 2030 solely to prevent production from falling. UKERC[35]

Low cost energy has been a cornerstone of long-term economic development throughout history. To state the obvious, energy and economic growth are positively correlated; surplus energy enables growth.

The price trend of oil can often be difficult to discern due to volatility. So rather than engaging in what I believe is a futile exercise of attempting to predict the exact price of oil next week, next quarter or even next year, I want to try to address two fundamental questions:

- What is the long-term downside to real oil prices from a further economic contraction?
- What is the long term upside to real oil prices from growth in the emerging economies?

Research from Cambridge Energy Research Associates provides the answer to the first question. By comparing the cost of production of the various sources of supply that make up current daily production volumes, you find that demand would have to drop by approximately 15 million barrels per day ("bbls/day") - around 20% of daily consumption - to create sustained US$ 60 per barrel prices. The reason for this is straightforward - the seventy million remaining barrels of daily supply would be unprofitable below this price. Of course, few industry analysts are forecasting large demand drops for now, certainly not on the order of magnitude required to create sustained US$ 60 per barrel oil prices again.

Obviously, it is the cost of the marginal barrel of oil that sets prices at any given level of demand. According to recent analysis by Bernstein in 2011, the marginal cost per barrel was US$ 92 for the 50 largest listed oil and gas companies and was expected to reach US$ 100 per barrel in 2012. Unsurprisingly, Bernstein concluded that incremental barrel costs were rising because incremental oil supply comes from increasingly technically difficult areas such as deep water or the Arctic which results in *higher material costs and reduced productivity per well.* We are in an environment where the production costs of large amounts of incremental oil are very high (think offshore, shale gas, tight oil and oil sands) so prices must remain high, otherwise supply is shut-in and disappears due to lack of profitability.

What is receiving a significant amount of attention is the scale of the incremental energy demand globally - which has surprised most analysts in being both large and resilient over the last 3 years. Current projections are for global demand to increase from around 85-90 million bbls/day today to 110 million bbls/day by 2025. How much new supply must be found in order to offset current decline rates and satisfy new demand?

Let us engage in a simple thought experiment with the following assumptions: 25 million bbls/day new demand by 2025 and an average decline rate of all currently producing fields of 4% per year. Based on these assumptions, in the next 10 years we must find approximately 50 million bbls/day or approximately 5 Saudi Arabias: 25 million bbls/day to maintain supply; and 25 million bbls/day new demand.

Just how realistic is it to assume such large growth on the demand side given poor growth prospects in the West? The key is to avoid the western centric perspective on energy consumption. In its "Energy Outlook 2030", British Petroleum predicts that just a single merging market - China - could increase its consumption by 8 million bbls/day to 18 million bbls/day, overtaking the US as the world's biggest oil consumer. Factor in India, Malaysia, the Philippines, Pakistan, Indonesia and numerous other emerging markets representing over 2 billion people becoming middle class and new demand will be large. According to the report, the developing nations will account for 93% of global energy demand growth over the next 20 years.

More specifically, global per capita oil demand has been extremely steady at 2 litres per day for last 40 years, and while per capita demand in the OECD[36] has dropped modestly over last the 10 years, per capita oil demand in the rest of the world (ROW) has nearly tripled to more than 1 litre per day. In addition, the ROW's population has grown much faster than in the OECD - 1.85% v. 0.74% annually.[37]

The result of these trends is that the ROW's oil consumption has grown seven times faster than the OECD's - increasing from 14% of the world total in 1971 to approximately 40% today. Even if annual per capita oil demand growth rates to 2030 were assumed to be zero in the OECD and the ROW continued at its 1971-2008 historical rate (2.54% annually), by 2030 total oil demand will be 138 million bbls/day, bringing the ROW's per capita demand to almost 2 litres per day and its share of total world demand to 58%.[38]

Leaving the demand side, it is fair to ask if the idea of supply constrained oil markets is some form of Malthusian hysteria? Here are some quotes from the horse's mouth so-to-speak. In 2009, The Guardian published the following commentary originating from a senior source at the International Energy Agency ("IEA"): *"The IEA in 2005 was predicting oil supplies could rise as high as 120 million barrels a day by 2030 although it was forced to reduce this gradually to 116m and then 105m last year [2008]. The 120 million figure always was nonsense but even today's number is much higher than can be justified and the IEA knows this. Many inside the organization believe that maintaining oil supplies at even 90 million to 95 million barrels a day would be impossible but there are fears that panic could spread on the financial markets if the figures were brought down further."*

In addition, the IEA has been warning for years, given current tighter supply/demand balance and increasing decline rates, that a reduction in upstream oil investment causes future supply problems much more quickly than in the past. IEA Director Nobuo Tanaka stated: *"Sustained investment is needed mainly to combat the decline in output at existing fields, which will drop by almost 2/3 by 2030."* Tanaka recently predicted that global upstream spending had dropped US$ 90 billion, or 19%, during 2009 versus 2008 - the first decline in a decade.

If the financial crisis worsens, capital will be in short supply even for the energy sector, at exactly the time when even greater amounts of capital are required to keep production stable and growing. On top of this, volatile oil prices make it more difficult for producers to plan capital budgets and make investments. As global markets, including energy commodities, become more volatile, producers and investors tend to reduce risk, even if the supply/demand and price trends are in their favour.

Let us now delve into another aspect of oil prices that receives far too little attention in the mainstream media. The issues are rapidly depreciating fiat currencies and developed nations that, for the most part, must import large amounts of oil to satisfy domestic consumption and maintain an energy intensive way of life. For example, the US must import approximately 8 million bbls/day (around 10% of global output). How is it possible for western nations to pursue weak currency policies while remaining highly dependent on imports to satisfy domestic oil demand? Zero interest rate policies and their associated money supply expansions may yet serve to bail out the insolvent banking sector but will severely impact the western middle class way of life via escalating costs, especially for energy.

Channelling the spirit of Rudolf Havenstein, (the president of the Reichsbank who oversaw the German hyperinflation of 1921-1923), US Federal Reserve officials have been quoted saying that higher oil prices may be the catalyst for further quantitative easing. Translation: our central bankers are saying that they will need to print more money in order to pay our oil bills. The thought that it is the rampant debasement of the world's fiat currencies that is contributing to the rise in oil prices never seems to enter their minds.

Even if you doubt that supply constraints or nominal oil prices are an issue, I would argue that EROEI decay most certainly is. Perhaps you have not heard of EROEI. You can be forgiven if it is not a topic that is on the tip of your tongue with issues of sovereign insolvency, quantitative easing, and the like dominating the airwaves.

I feel confident that EROEI is an acronym that will receive much wider recognition over the next decade. So what is EROEI you ask? It stands for "Energy Return On Energy Invested". It takes energy to produce new energy; therefore it is constructive to understand how the input energy compares to the output energy. Why is EROEI important today? Because we are in the process of transitioning from high EROEI sources of energy to low EROEI sources - think Saudi Arabia versus the Alberta oil sands. Here are some highly approximate EROEI ratios for various energy sources[39]:

- 1970s oil & gas discoveries - 30 to 1
- Current conventional oil & gas discoveries - 20 to 1
- 1980 coal - 20 to 1
- Oil Sands - 5 to 1
- Tight Oil - 5 to 1
- Nuclear - 4 to 1
- Photovoltaics - 4 to 1
- Biofuels - 2 to 1

Current conventional liquids production is estimated to be around 85-90 million bbls/day. However a 90 million bbls/day oil production profile of high EROEI sources is very different from 90 million bbls/day of low EROEI sources. Effectively, the net energy left over to drive economic growth is significantly lower in the latter scenario.

Assuming today's 90 million bbls/day were subject to 1970s' EROEI numbers, that would mean 3 million bbls was used to produce the 90 million, leaving 87 million bbls to sustain growth. Assuming 100% biofuels, then this drops to only 45 million bbls/day to sustain growth. The farther down the list we must go to maintain supply, the worse the net energy situation becomes.

I believe an increasing dependence on "difficult" oil has some serious consequences for the global economy. The amount capable of being produced from a given resource - the ultimate recovery - will be reduced. This will make it more challenging to increase overall production even where resources remain theoretically abundant. The costs, both tangible and intangible, of extracting remaining resources will escalate in terms of the energy inputs required, which in turn will drive real energy prices upwards. Why do we care about this? Economic growth is in large part a result of surplus energy. It follows that a reduction in EROEI will support higher real energy prices at the same time that it restricts growth.

I believe a clear sign that global EROEI is declining is demonstrated by energy expenditures as a percentage of global GDP. Global energy expenditures have been estimated at US$ 5 trillion to US$ 7 trillion based on a US$ 60 to US$ 80/bbl oil price. The world economy in 2010 was US$ 63 trillion and so energy accounted for around 8% to 11% of the total – a significant increase from the 5% to 6% it averaged in the last century. I believe these changes are, in part, a reflection of a sustained shift in the real cost of energy. If the real cost of hydrocarbon energy is going to increase, then the real cost of other commodities will also increase as most have significant energy inputs. On balance, I believe the net result will be a transfer of wealth from commodity consumers to commodity producers.

Chapter 6:
Agriculture – Food, Feed, and Fuel

"Expensive food is likely to persist for years because 'agflation' is underpinned by long-running changes in diet that accompany the growing wealth of emerging economies." The Economist

"Agricultural production is simply not growing fast enough to meet demand." Credit Suisse First Boston

"If every person in China ate 2 extra eggs a week it would use all the grain that Canada produces to feed the chickens." [40]

Cereal crop consumption will double by 2028. [41]

China has only 8 percent of the world's fresh water to meet the needs of 22 percent of the world's people. [42]

In India, urban water demand is expected to double and industrial demand to triple by 2025. [43]

To support the diets of the 1.7 billion people that will be added to the global population by 2030 at today's average dietary water consumption would require 2,040 cubic kilometers of water per year—as much as the annual flow of 24 Nile Rivers. [44]

"The world's farmers will need to produce more food in the next 50 years than farmers have produced in total over the last 10,000 years." Monsanto

O ver the last decade, agricultural commodity prices have been experiencing consistent and strong upward pressure. The reasons for this are simple:

- Inelastic demand curve;
- Emerging market demand growth profile;
- Food, feed, and fuel;
- Energy inputs;
- Productivity growth plateau; and
- Water inputs.

Inelastic Demand Curve: Demand inelasticity is one of the compelling qualities of the agricultural commodity sector. A demand curve is said to be inelastic if the demand for the item changes proportionally less than the price changes.[45] Goods with inelastic demand curves tend to be recession resistant.

Demand Growth Profile: Another interesting quality of agricultural commodities is that demand growth is not uniform as GDP per capita increases. What I mean by this is that demand is significantly front-end loaded. As GDP per capita increases up to US$ 5,000, an economy experiences a disproportionate jump in energy and agricultural commodity consumption. This means that, although the emerging economies have many decades of growth in order to come anywhere remotely close to developed world standards of living, their growth in the medium term will have a disproportionately higher effect on energy and agricultural commodity demand.

Food, Feed and Fuel: Agricultural commodity prices have been strong because of an step change increase in the use of these commodities for *"food, feed, and fuel"*.

- Food: It takes approximately 500 years to create 1 inch of topsoil.[46] Compare this replacement rate with the fact that in the last 200 years US topsoil has dropped from 21 inches to 6 inches on average (7 billion tons of soil are lost to erosion each year).[47] Globally, arable land has been decreasing each year while population has been increasing, resulting in a quite consistent trend of declining arable land per capita.[48]
- Feed: Depending on the animal protein consumed, an emerging economy can almost double the amount of crops it consumes as it switches to a high meat diet due to the multiplier effect of feeding livestock.
- Fuel: Despite their current low EROEI, most major oil-consuming nations have set mandatory biofuel targets. Obviously, these targets have consequences for agricultural commodity prices. By my calculation, current targets alone commit over 400 million acres to biofuel production[49], which represents approximately 10% of all the arable land in the world.[50] Some quick facts to put biofuels into perspective: 1) more than a quarter of the total U.S. grain crop was turned into ethanol to fuel cars in 2009 – a process that has been described as "turning fertilizer into gasoline"; 2) the amount of grain processed into biofuels has tripled in the US since 2004; and 3) if the entire U.S. grain crop were converted to ethanol it would only supply 18% of U.S. automotive fuel needs.[51]

Energy Inputs: Another driver of agricultural commodity prices is the price of energy inputs. Modern agriculture depends heavily on the use of fossil fuels - for machinery, irrigation, fertilizers, herbicides, storage and transportation. Clearly if energy prices increase, food prices should on balance also increase. Here are just a few examples of that energy/food linkage:

- The US and Canada export million of tons of grain every year - grain that contains large quantities of nitrogen, phosphorus, and potassium. The ongoing export of grain would slowly deplete the soil if the nutrients were not replaced with energy intensive man-made fertilizers;
- Irrigation accounts for approximately 20% of US farm energy use and in water-constrained locales such as India, over half of all electricity is used to drive irrigation pumps.

Productivity Growth Plateau: Productivity growth in agriculture has been nothing short of amazing. There is some truth to the comment that every year is a record for agriculture – because it has to be. Through a combination of increased mechanization, fertilizer and irrigation usage, and genetic engineering to improve yields and drought tolerance, we have kept production in step with increasing food demand even though the land base tends to be stagnant or in decline.

What is less obvious is that this productivity growth has slowed over the past decade. In the mid-twentieth century growth rates easily exceeded 3% per annum, while rates now hover around 1%. Given the finite amount of land and the declining marginal utility of adding additional fertilizer and/or machinery, the easy productivity gains have largely been achieved and so the rate of production growth has been slowing at exactly the point that demand has been accelerating.

Water Inputs: Another agriculture return driver is water. The water/food linkage is discussed less than the energy/food linkage but awareness is growing. In addition to food and energy, as people in the emerging economies make the transition to western standards of living their water consumption rises dramatically.

It is estimated that by 2030 global water requirements will increase approximately 50% from 4,500 billion m3 to 6,900 billion m3. This is believed to be 40% above current accessible, reliable supply.[52] Agriculture accounts for approximately 71% of current water use, and will increase to 4,500 billion m3 by 2030. The key locations for agricultural water demand are India, Sub-Saharan Africa and China.[53]

In China and India, any increase in water requirements compounds already poor domestic supply situations. In these countries, the loss of irrigation capacity as water is diverted from agricultural use will require even greater reliance on the export markets. Why? Seventy percent of the grain produced in China comes from irrigated land, but it is seeing its irrigation supply reduced by the diversion of water from rivers and reservoirs to cities and industrial use and the depletion of underground supplies in aquifers.

By 2025, Chinese non-irrigation water consumption is expected to increase by 75% over 1995 levels, leaving less water available for irrigation and creating massive additional need to import food crops. It is important to note that farms cannot compete economically with factories for water. A thousand tons of water produces one ton of wheat, which has a market value of around US$ 300, whereas the same amount of water used in industry yields an estimated US$ 14,000 of output - 70 times as much.[54]

China is already facing water shortages. China's per capita water resources are 2,200 cubic meters, only 31% of the world average and ranking 110th globally. By 2030, China, with a population estimated to be 1.6 billion, will drop to 1,760 cubic meters per capita – almost 25% lower.[55]

What can water supplies tell us about agricultural returns? A region like the Canadian prairies is a massive net exporter of water but does so indirectly in a more cost-effective way, via crops. Therefore, growing water supply constraints in major food importing countries should increase the value of farmland in markets where water is in good supply.

CHAPTER 7:
THE END OF UNIFORM GLOBAL GROWTH

Emerging economies are not just the cleverly-named and widely-discussed BRICs (Brazil, Russian, India, China). Do not forget Malaysia, Vietnam, Thailand, Philippines, Indonesia, Pakistan and a host of other countries whose populations amount to an additional billion people.

China

- GDP: US$ 7 trillion
- Consumer demand is 35% of GDP
- Savings rate is 40% of household income [56]

US

- GDP: US$ 15 trillion
- Consumer demand is 70% of GDP
- Savings rate is 4% of household income[57]

The emerging economies are now larger in total purchasing power GDP[58] terms than the developed world and are expected to surpass the developed world on an absolute basis before 2020. Their growth is also increasingly dependent on trade amongst themselves rather than with the developed world.[59]

As investors, we have lived in a relatively benign world in the last two decades with declining interest rates and solid growth in virtually every part of the global economy. Such an environment allows virtually any investment strategy to generate returns. I believe that this benign environment is ending and that growth will not be uniform across the globe. Outside of the monetary issues that are discussed earlier in this book, the primary reason for this change is the West's increasing lack of fundamentals for growth:

- Aging populations, increasing dependency ratios;
- Large unfunded liabilities for social benefits;
- High total debt-to-GDP levels;
- Low savings rates;
- Increasing government intervention in the economy;
- Large fiscal deficits; and
- Overly accommodative monetary authorities.

By way of contrast, many emerging economies have the opposite characteristics:

- Favourable demographics, declining dependency ratios;
- Low national debt levels;
- High savings rates; and
- Competitive manufacturing bases.

It is this rise of the saving and investment driven emerging market competitors that is a serious threat to western economic hegemony. There is a virtuous cycle underway in the emerging economies - high growth rates combined with high savings rates create a large pool of domestic capital which fuels investment which in turn fuels further growth and savings (emerging market savings rates are often 20% or higher).

The results are strikingly apparent. First western manufacturing jobs were exported, but as the emerging economies develop they are moving into more white-collar sectors. The West is now also competing for the service jobs that represent the remaining 60%-70% of its economy. It should be no surprise that technology is providing the mechanism for this development. For just a few data points think of outsourced radiology analysis and accounting audits conducted via inexpensive high-speed communications and intelligent software programs doing legal work.

The result of all this has been to accelerate growth in the developing world while simultaneously impeding growth in large segments of the developed world. To give an example of what I mean, I will use Canada. Canada is evolving into a "two-track" bifurcated economy. Growth trends are very different in the East versus the West. Western Canada has been growing at approximately twice the rate as eastern Canada over the last decade.

Eastern Canada, represented by Ontario and Quebec, is heavily exposed to deteriorating US fundamentals through its automotive and aerospace industries. To put it simply, Eastern Canada imports what the emerging economies need and exports what they make, putting it under pressure on both the cost and revenue side of the equation.

Meanwhile western Canada, represented by British Columbia, Alberta and Saskatchewan, is in the enviable position of exporting what the emerging economies need and importing what they make. What do I mean by this? It is a well-understood process that energy and food consumption undergo rapid growth as a developing economy makes the transition to a middle class standard of living. Energy and agriculture are western Canada's dominant industries and, with only 10 million inhabitants, domestic demand for these commodities is relatively low.

Therefore, western Canada is one of the world's major net exporters of both energy and agricultural commodities. It is because of this that investments in western Canada have, to a material degree, captured higher emerging economy growth rates and that the western Canadian provinces have consistently outperformed those in the East.

CHAPTER 8:
THE RETREAT OF FINANCIALIZATION

"Imprudent granting of credit is bound to prove just as ruinous to a bank as to any other merchant." Ludwig von Mises

"What is needed for a sound expansion of production is additional capital goods, not money or fiduciary media. The credit boom is built on the sands of banknotes and deposits. It must collapse."
Ludwig von Mises

The First Bank of North America, the first US central bank, was chartered in 1781 and failed only 3 years later in 1784.

Nearly the entire global market in derivatives is dominated by just five firms: JP Morgan Chase, Goldman Sachs, Bank of America, Citibank, and Wells Fargo.[60]

I do not adhere to the belief that banking is intrinsically "bad". Banking and finance serve a productive purpose in the economy by intermediating savings and investments. However, I believe that what passes for much of modern banking (or more accurately post-1971 banking with its dysfunctional central bank/private bank nexus and its anti-competitive nature courtesy of regulatory barriers to entry) is not productive and is actually acting as an impediment to the economy by destroying vast amounts of real capital through bailouts and mal-investments.

So with that context in mind, I believe it is putting it mildly indeed to say that we have arrived at a point where the vast majority of financial institutions are simply regulatory oligopolies with asset-harvesting business models more concerned with fees and proprietary speculative activities than with providing any useful services to savers and retail investors. On the issue of what value recent financial sector activities and innovations have created, Paul Volcker, the former Chairman of the US Federal Reserve, stated *"the only useful* [recent] *banking innovation was the invention of the ATM."*

The mainstream financial sector has indoctrinated an entire generation to diversify and to "buy and hold" because it suits their business model that is asset-driven rather than performance-driven. Large financial firms have an intrinsic institutional bias to be bullish on everything. They have no incentive to tell you not to invest in something, as they will usually be operating a fund in that area. Hence their analysts use such sophistry as being *"underweight"* unattractive asset classes rather than encouraging outright selling. Ultimately, they have little investment insight other than the view that everything will go up in the long run. Of course, in the long run, it has been quipped that we are all dead. To add insult to injury, the financial sector seldom outperforms the benchmarks over long periods and charge management fees for what is effectively closet indexing.

Once again, I am not a knee-jerk critic of the financial sector but I do believe that it has become too large and, in part, may now represent a net impediment rather than a net contributor to the economy. Corporate profits attributable to the US finance sector were effectively stable from the 1950s to the early 1980s from 5% to 15%. Then, as the growth in the money supply turned sharply higher on a sustained basis in the 1980s, profits peaked at more than 40% in the early 2000s and still remain around 30% - substantially higher than long term averages.

On an asset basis the numbers tell a similar story. The 20 largest banks in the US have combined assets of approximately 90% of US GDP. The five largest banks - JPMorgan Chase, Bank of America, Citigroup, Wells Fargo, and Goldman Sachs - have combined assets of approximately 60% of US GDP. These numbers are roughly 4 times what they were in the 1990s. [61]

Given the finance sector's intimate relationship with government and central banks, it is not surprising that it grows faster than the underlying economy. Newly-printed money flows into and through the finance sector acting as a wholesale subsidy that supports corporate profits, compensation, and speculation. Despite widespread belief to the contrary, government intervention into broad swathes of the financial sector to support *"too big to fail"* banks or, more accurately, to prevent capital-destroying business activity from being eliminated, is not a positive for future growth. When it is funded via expansionary monetary policy, at best it is laying the groundwork for stagflation.

There is an economic truism that you get more of whatever you subsidize. Hence, by subsidizing failure we are ensuring bigger failures in the future and, worst of all, penalizing well-run businesses. The firms that were prudently managed leading up to the crisis should have benefited from the demise of their poorly run competitors. In a free economy, capital would have flowed to the profitable businesses rather than the loss-making ones. The fact that this did not happen creates a perverse *"if you can't beat'em, join'em"* mentality with respect to risky and imprudent business practices.

Let us be clear on one thing, the primary purpose of low interest rates is not to save the economy, it is to save the politically connected banks and allow them to continue their risky, bonus-generating behavior. Low interest rates are simply a case of robbing Peter to pay Paul, as capital is being *"strip-mined"* from savers via low interest rates and in effect *"donated"* to the financial sector.

For example, how much are taxpayers subsidizing Canadian banks? Assume CAD$ 1 trillion of deposits with regulated financial institutions and that interest rates are 3% below long-term averages due to Bank of Canada intervention in the markets. The result is an implicit CAD$ 30 billion/year subsidy to the Canadian banking sector. Now multiply this process across the entire developed world and the magnitude of the wealth transfer from savers to banks starts to be apparent.

I would argue that the enormous size of the financial sector coupled with its current insolvency (or massive undercapitalization at best), which the constant bail-outs are attempting to disguise, will be a drag on growth for years unless losses are allowed to take place via write downs and liquidations. Sadly, more bailouts are certain to take place in the financial sector because it has the political influence to compel the state to commandeer capital from other more healthy parts of the economy and monetize their losses. Without even trying to speculate on the hidden sources of losses hiding away in the dark corners of bank balance sheets, there are huge exposures right in front of us in the form of commercial real estate loans, non-sovereign state debt (e.g. municipal and state bonds), student loans and sovereign debt (an asset class that is rapidly changing from the world's "risk free return" asset to its "return free risk" asset).

In addition to the elevated level of corporate profits accruing to the financial sector, two other interesting indicators of the financialization of western economies are: 1) the ratio of the Commodities Research Bureau Spot Index[62] versus the S&P 500; and 2) notional global derivatives[63] value to global GDP. Put another way, these ratios are rough indicators of the growth of financial assets in relation to real assets, so to speak.

CRB versus S&P 500: The long-term average of this ratio has been around 1.5 times. Simplistically, this ratio indicates how much S&P 500 stock you can buy with a fixed basket of commodities:

- 1970s: During the commodity bull market of the 1970s, the ratio was consistently higher than 2 times and peaked at around 4 times.
- 2012: The ratio is currently around 0.3 times - far below the 1.5 times long-term average and far below the 4 times peak seen in the last commodity bull market.

Notional Derivatives Value versus Global GDP: The notional value of derivatives in existence versus GDP gives another indication of the growth of the financial sector in relation to the underlying economy.

- 2002: Total OTC derivatives to Global GDP ratio approximately 3 times
- 2012: Total OTC derivatives to Global GDP ratio approximately 10 times[64][65][66]

Over the course of a decade, the Over-The-Counter ("OTC") derivatives market has tripled to 10 times the size of the underlying, real global economy – arguably with little benefit other than transaction fees for financial institutions or, more cynically, the ability in the short-term to book phantom profits through the use of mark-to-model valuations on these opaque, non-publically traded instruments.

I would not suggest that the indicators above will be perfectly predictive of how the financial sector will fare going forward, but they are certainly food for thought as we appear to be at an all-time low relative valuation between "real assets" and "financial assets." To say that the process of financialization will tend to retreat rather than grow from here is simply another way of saying that the ratio of real assets to financial assets will return to something closer to its long-term average. If history is a guide, the impetus for this reversion will be investors seeking safety outside of the insolvent private and public financial systems.

Chapter 9:
Anticipate and Prosper

"The average long-term experience in investing is never surprising, but the short term experience is always surprising." Charles Ellis

"The four most dangerous words in investing are 'This time it's different.'" John Templeton

"There are no new eras - excesses are never permanent." Bob Farrell

"Simplicity is the ultimate sophistication." Leonardo Da Vinci

"Sometimes the law defends plunder and participates in it. Sometimes the law even places the whole apparatus of judges, police, prisons and gendarmes at the service of the plunderers, and treats the victim, when he defends himself, as a criminal...But often the masses are plundered and do not even know it." Frédéric Bastiat

"How did you go bankrupt? Two ways. Gradually, then suddenly." Ernest Hemingway

Western governments are hopelessly addicted to deficit financing – a practice in which a government spends more money than it receives as revenue. The difference is made up by borrowing or printing new money while refusing to address looming funding issues.

"In some ways it's a battle of the politicians against the markets. That's how I do see it. But I'm determined to win this battle." Angela Merkel

With apologies to the embarrassingly misguided Angela Merkel who, at the time of writing is Chancellor of Germany, politicians can no more successfully "battle" the markets than you and I can successfully "battle" gravity. How long will governments continue to ignore the fact that countries, like people, can and do go bankrupt - often quite suddenly as Mr. Hemingway reminds us.

Keynesian deficit and money printing economic policies are now being pursued globally on a scale without precedent. If history is a guide, printing modest amounts of money creates modest amounts of inflation and printing large amounts of money creates large amounts of inflation. Central banks have an almost unbroken track record of being able to devalue their currencies and create inflation. I believe that this episode will be no different.

Where does intervention in the economy by western governments through bailouts and money supply expansions leave us?

By subsidizing failure and creating even greater moral hazard, the bailouts will increase the amount of mispriced risk in the system - not reduce it. The financial sector has barely begun the process of recognizing and accurately provisioning for existing losses and, rest assured, ZIRP will create a host of new problems. Problems are likely to arise on a scale and in ways that we cannot foresee today - the law of unintended consequences will not be denied. Ask yourself what unsound risks are being taken onto bank, hedge fund, corporate and personal balance sheets today because long-term funding rates are under 3% in many cases?

At the highest level, central banks are now aggressively monetizing government deficits. The mechanism is simple - recipient banks take the newly-printed money they receive in exchange for their badly impaired assets and buy sovereign debt. Indirect monetization to be sure, but money is fungible so monetization nonetheless. I would also argue that this monetization is an explicit policy objective. If so, now that central banks are rid of the philosophical hesitation to print the money to fund government financing shortfalls, what is left to stop them from any amount of printing, for any purpose?

This type of money supply expansion historically has been strongly inflationary. Many would argue that we see no evidence of that effect in this episode, in fact quite the opposite, that we're in a deflationary environment.

But to interpret price declines in select asset classes as deflation misses the underlying issue entirely. Heavily leveraged asset classes - e.g. banks, sovereign debt, residential and commercial real estate – will continue to suffer nominal price declines while solvency remains an issue and their access to credit is reduced. This is not the same as a general falling of prices throughout the economy.

Money/credit will continue to flow out of these overleveraged and falling asset classes and move into new areas of the economy - likely those sectors whose fundamentals remain unimpaired and where debt levels are moderate. Real assets, such as gold and commodities, appear to be among the logical candidates.

Meanwhile, faced with the lack of organic growth to fix their problems, western politicians are hoping for Keynesian monetary policy to artificially stimulate growth. The top-line is often the simplest thing to change in any projection and politicians are availing themselves of this "fix". I do not believe the amount of growth required will be forthcoming because the recovery in the West is not being built on the sound fundamentals for growth outlined in the previous chapters:

- Favourable demographics;
- Low national debt levels;
- High savings rates; and
- Competitive manufacturing bases.

By insisting on printing over the systemic solvency issues in the financial sector, by actively preventing the liquidation of decades of mal-investment, by subsidizing speculation and consumption to the detriment of production, and so on, central bankers will not create a recovery. They are creating an inflationary environment with poor prospects for real growth - i.e. stagflation.

The emerging economies have most, if not all, of the favourable growth components and are still experiencing a once-in-a-lifetime industrialization process and the birth of a middle class.

Sadly, the developed world's largest export seems to have become fiat currency. With few exceptions, the West is following expansionary monetary policies and running large current account deficits, most often with the developing world.

As a consequence, most emerging economies operate mercantilist foreign exchange policies – striving to reduce the value of their currencies against those of their western export partners. China in particular seeks to maintain its peg against inherently weak western currencies by accumulating foreign exchange reserves and printing the local currency - the Renminbi. Though increasingly demonized in the western media, the Renminbi peg has acted as an inflation-importing mechanism - without which inflation would be rising even faster in the West due to our profligate monetary and fiscal policies. When China decides to loosen or eliminate the peg - inflation in the West will surely receive an unwelcome boost. In the meantime, China is balancing the utility of using the Renminbi peg to fuel domestic industrialization against the cost of importing western (primarily US) inflation that impoverishes Chinese citizens with an artificially devalued currency. The Chinese government is beginning to face the domestic inflation problems inherent in its strategy and is trying to take steps to reduce that inflation without adjusting the peg – akin to trying to have your cake and eat it too. It remains to be seen how this will turn out.

In an environment such as this, the issue is not how high real assets like gold can rise; rather, it is how low fiat currencies can fall. If you believe that gold prices, like most real assets, are rising because gold is being remonetized then its ultimate price is dictated by how much further fiat currencies will be devalued. Here is an interesting valuation methodology assuming some form of full remonetization: determine what gold price is necessary for each unit of central bank paper to be backed by that country's gold reserves. If, for example, you perform this calculation for the US using M1 as the monetary numerator you obtain the following results:

- Gold reserves - 8,133 tonnes, M1 - US$ 1.8 trillion = gold price of approximately US$ 6,900/oz

In the spirit of the whimsical but alarming, I will repeat this calculation for the EU, the UK and Canada:

- EU – 10,792 tonnes, M1 - €1.1 trillion = approximate gold price/oz €3,200
- UK – 310 tonnes, M1 - £4.7 trillion = approximate gold price/oz £472,000
- Canada – 3 tonnes, M1 CAD$ 0.5 trillion = approximate gold price /oz CAD$ 5,200,000

Canada is conspicuous in its low gold reserves – in both absolute and relative terms. Therefore, a move to a new *de jure* gold standard might have far greater consequences for the Canadian dollar. If gold were to be re-monetized, the Canadian dollar would face an almost 100% devaluation in order to be backed by Canada's current gold reserves. Granted, this is a simplistic thought experiment that ignores many factors, including the effect of the gold holdings of foreign fiat currencies held by the Bank of Canada as reserves, but it is interesting nonetheless given the market perception of the soundness of the Canadian dollar.

In this hostile financial climate, investors must now give more thought than ever to long-term capital preservation first and sustainable growth second. Growth is not sustainable if it is driven by debt-fuelled consumption. You must ensure your return of capital, not your return on capital. Take Canada as an example of a potential market for investment. It can be argued that Canada suffers from many of the problems of the typical developed nation outlined in the preceding chapters, though to a lesser degree than its G8 brethren. Canada is the best of the worst, so to speak. Still, it has familiar developed-economy problems.

This raises the question: why should investors emphasize investments in developed economies such as Canada over emerging economies? The fact is that direct investments in emerging economies often come with higher levels of political risk. Argentina's expropriation of oil assets and its punitive export tariffs on agricultural commodities during its 2008 food crisis is an informative example.

Political risk as it relates to commodities will be an even greater issue going forward. Most of the world's critical commodities – energy and food - are found in politically unstable regions of the world. I believe that, as governments grow increasingly desperate for capital to prop up impaired financial and entitlement systems, the risk of expropriation will rise further.

As a consequence of rising political risk premiums, investors will be forced to focus on commodity-rich regions in the developed markets that combine emerging market growth profiles with politically stability, even if these markets represent more mature asset bases. Assets in such markets may attract a premium to those in countries that are more hostile to foreign capital. That is the investment draw of Canada. Even though it faces many of the issues of the rest of the developed world, there is an opportunity to capture emerging market returns in Canada due to its uniquely bifurcated economy.

Volatility will also continue at elevated levels while the West experiences strong inflationary forces at the same time as the liquidation of decades of mal-investments.[67] Therefore:

- Avoid investments in sectors that have high overall debt levels and/or inferior cash-generating capability;

- We are now in a highly selective investing market – expect asset class returns to diverge significantly; and
- *"Dart board"* investing, where everything increases in value, is over.

There are many credible analysts who are predicting deflation at the same time as others are predicting inflation. As investors, how do you even begin to position yourself in a world of such diametrically opposite outcomes? In the short term, I believe it might be useful to view the world as having a barbell shaped distribution of possible outcomes. The barbell is meant to be a simplistic visual representation of a portfolio that, at its core (handle), has strong capital preservation qualities, with one side having high impact positions for a deflationary world and the other side, high impact positions for an inflationary world.

If we muddle through, the dominant capital preserving core (handle) leaves the investor with the bulk of his capital intact. In an inflationary world, the deflation investments are lost but the inflation investments make up the loss and generate positive returns. The outcome, of course, is inverted for a deflationary world.

How can I even recommend positioning for deflation? As I view deflation strictly as a shrinking money supply – perhaps it is better to say that I recommend positioning for a generalized and widespread drop in certain prices with an attendant temporary increase in the value of cash and cash equivalents as financial assets and collateral are liquidated. For me this is a 2-stage process:

- Stage 1 is a wide scale move out of financial assets causing sharp price declines that in turn are interpreted as a deflationary event; and
- Stage 2 is the policy response, accelerating the growth of monetary aggregates and pushing them into the banking system in any way possible to shore up solvency.

This, in turn, will create inflation, which as Cantillon has clearly demonstrated, is not an aggregate or neutral phenomenon. The *"too big to fail"* banks will get the new money first and even state-subsidized bankers do not like to make losses. Therefore, I believe that there will come a point when even newly-printed money will make a pronounced migration out of financial assets and into real assets. The drivers for the scenario above are not hard to conceptualize:

- Deteriorating finances of the public sector;
- Monetary authorities willing to fill the gap by printing money;
- Low real growth rates in the West; and
- Higher real growth in the emerging economies.

It follows from all that has been discussed here that over the short term you need to increase the "robustness" of your portfolio: increase your cash and cash equivalents; and avoid using leverage or margin either directly or indirectly.

In the longer term:

- Identify and perhaps reduce investments that are overly reliant on real growth in western markets;
- Consider investments in sectors that are directly exposed to emerging economy growth in politically stable parts of the world;
- Invest to eliminate or reduce counterparty risk – e.g. physical precious metals versus ETFs, farmland versus corn futures etc. As a passive investor you will never be compensated sufficiently to take counter-party risk; and
- Invest in assets classes whose products have inelastic demand curves.

For those who are uninterested in making investment decisions in the current environment, I would recommend that, at the bare minimum, you consider the following:

- Intellectual Capital: You need to avoid being the median worker in the West at all costs. The median worker is most exposed to competition from the emerging markets. Focus on your intellectual capital. Continually strive to build unique, high value skills; otherwise, your only competitive advantage in the global market for services may be price. For those able to compete on skills, the rewards will be significant – it is becoming a "winner takes all" global economy.
- Purchasing Power: Protect the purchasing power of your savings and assets – capital losses will be very difficult to recover in a ZIRP world without taking material risk.
- Retirement Funding: Start building your retirement capital now if you have not already – do not rely on the government.
- Consumption: Under-consume and over-save. Remember that consumption represents the destruction of capital.

Epilogue

It seems apparent to me that, outside the hallowed halls of government, central banks and *"too big to fail"* financial institutions, there is a growing realization about the scope of problems we face and that the aforementioned entities just might be the culprits who created them.

Often we are unable to be objective about current events. If we were to look on the current global fiat money supply expansion and massive bail-outs of insolvent banks and sovereign states as something that took place 200 years ago, these actions would be roundly condemned as counter-productive and likely to lead to a massive loss of purchasing power of the currencies involved, at the very least. Yet we raise no such concerns today, simply, it seems, because we are immersed in these events in real-time and nothing truly terrible has happened…yet.

Remember that in the historic examples of such behaviour, events moved discontinuously – even as the money supply mounted no crises seemed to happen with the currency, the financial sector, or with the state's ability to borrow and spend with virtually no limit. Then suddenly, one day, everything changed at once.

Do not expect events to unfold gradually – the amount of money involved in the global financial system and the speed with which it can move will make the endgame very sudden and most likely quite unexpected.

What is that end game? It is not a secret what causes inflation. It is not a secret what enriches the political and banking classes to the detriment of all others. It is not a secret what impoverishes savers and the middle class. It is not a secret what destroys the purchasing power of a currency.

We are putting in place all of the necessary pre-conditions for some very poor outcomes. Just because nothing bad has happened is not proof that nothing bad is going to happen. Surely history is stocked with sufficient examples of why current policies are a bad idea that we should not be forced by governments and central bankers to live through another episode.

I must say I am not optimistic on this front but perhaps events will surprise me.

Acknowledgements

My thanks are owed to a large number of people who offered advice, insight and undertook the tedious task of trying to edit my thoughts. Of course the errors and misjudgements within are mine alone.

I am indebted to Kenton Toews who performed the difficult task of the first edit. Redmond Weissenberger and the Mises Institute of Canada for acting as publisher. Richard Veldhoen whose enthusiasm and encouragement kept me engaged through the many months of drafting. My brother and sister, Ricki and Matthew Johnston, who provided invaluable input in Austrian thought and English grammar… not, it must be said, without a certain amount of cajoling. Daron Naffin who, in addition to being a dab hand at editing, is a not inconsiderable wine connoisseur. Last, but certainly not least, Naomi Nind for her perfectionism - a quality that was much appreciated.

Stephen Johnston

Recommended Reading

If you have not already, please take the time to read these books. I am confident they will cast some light on our current economic problems:

- *The Dying of Money* by Jens Parssons
- *The Law* by Frederic Bastiat
- *Economics in One Lesson* by Henry Hazlitt
- *What Has Government Done to Our Money?* by Murray Rothbard
- *The Road to Serfdom* by Friederich von Hayek
- *Freedom and Capitalism* by Milton Friedman
- *The Pretense of Knowledge* by Friedrich von Hayek
- *Human Action* by Ludwig von Mises
- *America's Great Depression* by Murray Rothbard
- *The Black Swan* & *Fooled By Randomness* by Nassim Taleb
- *The (Mis) Behavior of Markets* by Benoit Mandelbrot
- *Man, Economy, and State* by Murray Rothbard

About the Author

Stephen Johnston is the founder of a family of alternative investment funds. Over his career Stephen has managed both private equity and debt investments – with roles at the European Bank for Reconstruction and Development, Société Générale Asset Management – Emerging Europe and Baring Brothers among others. Stephen created one of the first farmland investment funds in Canada.

Stephen has a BSc. (1987) and an LLB (1990) from the University of Alberta and an MBA (1994) from the London Business School. Stephen is a frequent guest on BNN and his analysis of the financial markets and alternative investments has appeared in a wide range of media outlets including Macleans, the Financial Times, Canadian Business magazine and the Globe and Mail.

About the Publisher

Ludwig von Mises Institute of Canada: The Mises Institute of Canada was founded in 2010 to spread the teachings of the Austrian School of Economics. It is the mission of the Institute to educate the Canadian public on the importance of placing human choice at the center of economic theory, to encourage a revival of critical historical research, and to advance the Misesian tradition of thought through the defense of the market economy, private property, sound money, and peaceful international relations. For more information email contact@mises.ca.

Bibliography
(Endnotes)

1   Keynesian economics are based on the ideas of John Maynard Keynes. Keynesians believe that, in the short run, productive activity is influenced by aggregate demand (total spending in the economy), and that aggregate demand does not necessarily equal aggregate supply – roughly speaking the idea that some form of output gap can arise. Advocates of Keynesian economics argue that the private sector sometimes creates inefficient macroeconomic outcomes that require intervention by the state to stabilize output over the business cycle. The theories forming the basis of Keynesian economics were first presented by Keynes in his book, *The General Theory of Employment, Interest and Money*, published in 1936. Obviously, Keynesians advocate a large role for government intervention during recessions to "stimulate demand".

2   Stagflation is an economic environment where the inflation rate is high, economic growth is low and unemployment is high. Stagflation is poorly understood by Keynesians because inflation and recession were regarded as mutually exclusive in that school of thought – a view that was subsequently shown to be false.

3   Fiat money is money whose use and value government regulation or law dictates – typically in reference to un-backed paper currencies rather than commodity monies. Fiat is Latin for *"let it be done"*. I will be using fiat currency/fiat money throughout this book to mean non-redeemable paper currency (i.e. paper currency that is not backed by gold).

4   St Louis Federal Reserve, Monetary Base (M0) growth

5   Ibid.

6   Fannie Mae - The Federal National Mortgage Association is a government-sponsored enterprise (GSE). Fannie Mae's mandate is to expand the secondary mortgage market by securitizing mortgages in the form of mortgage-backed securities (MBS), allowing lenders to reinvest their assets into more lending and, in effect, increasing the number of lenders in the mortgage market by reducing the reliance on thrifts. Freddie Mac - The Federal Home Loan Mortgage Corporation (FHLMC), is a GSE. Freddie Mac was created in 1970 to expand the secondary market for mortgages in the US. Freddie Mac buys mortgages on the secondary market, pools them, and sells them as a mortgage-backed security to investors on the open market. Freddie Mac and Fannie Mae were instrumental in creating the real estate bubble in the US via below market mortgage rates and became insolvent when the market crashed in 2008.

7   On August 15, 1971, President Richard Nixon announced that the U.S. would no longer officially trade US dollars for gold, signalling the end of the partial gold standard (gold exchange standard established by the Bretton Woods Agreement) that had existed since 1946. The basis of this partial standard was the US fixing the price of gold at US$ 35/ounce and signatories to Bretton Woods pegging their currencies to the US dollar. Foreign holders of US dollars could exchange for gold at the fixed rate of US$ 35/ounce.

8   J.P. Morgan, testifying to Congress in 1912

9   Foreign Exchange Rates: The price of a currency expressed in another country's currency – therefore the relative rate at which one currency can be exchanged for another.

10 Estimated as of 2012

11 Negative nominal interest rates mean that instead of earning interest on your deposit, you are charged interest – i.e. the value of your deposit declines rather than grows over time.

12 Marc Faber

13 Laurence Kotlikoff

14 Morgan Stanley, Sovereign Subjects, "Ask Not Whether Governments Will Default, but How." August 25, 2010

15 Jordan Roy-Byrne

16 Popular Delusions, "Some Useful Things I've Learned About Germany's Hyperinflation," SG Cross Asset Research, Dylan Grice

17   "TMS counts only immediately available money for exchange and does not double count. MMMF shares are excluded from TMS because they represent equity shares in a portfolio of highly liquid, short-term investments which must be sold in exchange for money before such shares can be redeemed. For a more detailed description and explanation of the TMS aggregate, see Salerno (1987) and Shostak (2000). The TMS consists of the following: Currency Component of M1, Total Checkable Deposits, Savings Deposits, U.S. Government Demand Deposits and Note Balances, Demand Deposits Due to Foreign Commercial Banks, and Demand Deposits Due to Foreign Official Institutions."

18   Shadowstats.org
19   Laurence Kotlikoff
20   IMF working paper - "An Analysis of U.S. Fiscal and Generational Imbalances: Who Will Pay and How?"
21   "The real effects of debt", Cecchetti, Mohanty und Zampolli, Bank for International Settlements, August 2011
22   Statscan
23   Northern Trust, It's More Than Just the Numbers, Demographic Shifts & Investment Strategies, June 2010

24   Bank of America – The Longest Picture June 2012

25   Boomer Retirement: Headwinds for U.S. Equity Markets? FRBSF Economic Letter, August 2011

26   Kellogg School of Management
27   Mark-to-market refers to accounting for the "fair value" of an asset or liability based on the current market price.
28   Center for Retirement Research at Boston College - "How Would GASB Proposals Affect State and Local Pension Reporting?"
29   Society of Certified General Accountants, Gauging the Path of Private Canadian Pensions: 2010 Update on the State of Defined Benefit and Defined Contribution Pension Plans
30   Ibid.
31   Standard and Poor's
32   Mike Hewitt – DollarDaze.org
33   UK Energy Research Centre, www.ukerc.ac.uk
34   Ibid.
35   Ibid.
36   Organisation for Economic Co-Operation and Development
37   Joyce Dargay and Dermot Gately
38   Ibid.
39   The methodology for calculating EROEI is still in its infancy. There is considerable variance amongst the practitioners as to how to take into account the multitude of factors that can affect the results – for example cleanup costs, waste storage, transportation etc. EROEI numbers should be treated with a certain caution and be used to provide a general overview of the direction of the global net energy supply only.
40   Worldwatch
41   Ibid.
42   Ibid.
43   Ibid.
44   Ibid.

45   A demand curve is said to be inelastic if the demand for the item changes proportionately less than the price changes – e.g. a 10% price increase only causes a 1% drop in demand. Demand curves for items that people need to survive, such as staple foods or energy, tend to be inelastic because, within reason, people will buy such goods regardless of price.

46   US Department of Agriculture - NRCS

47 Soil Erosion: A Food and Environmental Threat, David Pimentel, Journal of the Environment, Development and Sustainability (Vol. 8, 2006)

48 Agcapita Farmland Investment Partnership data

49 Based on current bio-ethanol technology

50 Agcapita Farmland Investment Partnership data

51 Worldwatch

52 McKinsey & Company

53 Ibid.

54 Earth Policy Institute, Lester Brown

55 Ibid.

56 Washington Post, "Getting Chinese to stop saving and start spending is a hard sell", July 2012, World Bank, China Daily, "Private consumption to take up 45% of GDP by 2015" March 2011

57 Washington Post, Getting Chinese to stop saving and start spending is a hard sell, July 2012, World Bank

58 Purchasing power parity (PPP) GDP allows you to compare GDP between countries by taking into account the impact of their exchange rates and therefore the relative costs of goods and services in each country.

59 Emerging vs. Developed Economies, Power Shift, The Economist, August 2011 & Canadian Business, Business Without Borders, June 2012

60 Comptroller of the Currency - www.occ.gov/topics/capital-markets/financial-markets/trading/derivatives/dq211.pdf

61 St. Louis Federal Reserve, www.politifact.com/truth-o-meter/statements/2010/apr/27/sherrod-brown/six-largest-banks-getting-bigger-brown-said

62 Commodity Research Bureau Spot Commodities Index "is a measure of price movements of 22 sensitive basic commodities whose markets are presumed to be among the first to be influenced by changes in economic conditions."

63 A derivative is a financial contract between parties whose value is based on one or more underlying assets. Such contracts stipulate terms (typically dates, resulting values of the underlying variables, and notional amounts) under which payments are to be made between the parties.

64 Bank of International Settlements – Derivatives Data

65 Bank of England, "OTC derivatives reform and collateral demand impact", October 2012

66 Over-the-counter: Derivatives that do not trade on an exchange, dealing is done between the counterparties directly.

67 On the topic of volatility, it is worth noting that before 1972 commodity prices were highly stable. The Commodity Research Bureau Index (a basket of commodities) traded close to 100 from its inception in the early 1950s to 1972. In 1971 the US defaulted on its international obligation to redeem dollars for gold, severing the last vestiges of the gold standard. The rate of growth of the US money supply has accelerated consistently since this event and, along with it, the nominal prices of virtually everything began to exhibit elevated volatility.